PATIENCE

by
Richard F. Clarke, SJ

*All booklets are published thanks to the
generous support of the members of the
Catholic Truth Society*

CATHOLIC TRUTH SOCIETY
PUBLISHERS TO THE HOLY SEE

CONTENTS

Patience and Suffering

Patience and Impatience

Temptation

Examples of Patience

Fruits of Patience

PATIENCE AND SUFFERING

What is Patience?

Patience is the willing endurance of what is painful to us. It is a very necessary virtue if we wish to pass happily through life. "Patience", says the heathen poet, "lightens every suffering that cannot be avoided." Those who are naturally patient have a far more pleasant time of it than the irritable and impatient. Patience is therefore a virtue worth cultivating quite apart from any motives of religion. Like all else that is good, it smoothes the rugged path of life. Have I not learned by experience that it is a blessed gift which they who lack have to suffer miseries unknown to the patient?

The virtue of patience consists in the willing endurance for God's sake of all that is painful to nature, of whatever kind it may be. It has for its subject-matter physical as well as moral and spiritual suffering. It teaches us to bear patiently bodily pains, poverty and sickness, as well as sorrow, desolation, loss of friends, unkindness, misrepresentation, insult, ingratitude, injury, persecutions, contempt, neglect. It submits without complaint to all the words and actions of others that jar upon us and cause us pain. In one or other of these ways, and perhaps in many, I have to suffer. Am I patient?

The field for patience is a wide one. There is no lack of opportunities for its exercise. For most, a day rarely passes without some call upon our patience; as long as we are in this vale of tears, suffer we must. Grant me patience, O my God, since I am surrounded with occasions in which I have need of it. Grant that I may love it and practise it for love of You!

The Need of Patience

This life is indeed a vale of tears. Trouble of every kind surrounds us; trouble from without, trouble from within, trouble for our bodies, trouble for our souls; trouble coming upon us most unexpectedly and sometimes lasting for years; troubles temporal and troubles spiritual; troubles quite unmerited and troubles that come to us through our own fault. No one can escape from trouble. "Man that is born of a woman hath but a short life and is full of sorrow." How strange it seems that men cling to a life so full of trouble! O my God, we ought to thank You that this life is so short and eternity so long.

Yet every trouble is sent in mercy, and is intended by our Father in Heaven to help us on our road there. They are the means of our probation; they test whether we are the children of God. If we bear them with patience we shall be saved; it is only if we rebel against them and refuse to submit to them that they are really evils and misfortunes to us. Everything depends on our good-will. What is my attitude to the troubles that God sends me?

There are few virtues for which there is such continual necessity as patience. The occasions requiring its exercise are manifold indeed. Whatever our position and our work, our patience is sure to be constantly tried. Generally the trial is one that comes suddenly upon us, and unless we are on our guard, the impatient look or gesture escapes us before we are conscious of it. It takes a long time to overcome those first movements of impatience which, though they are half voluntary or involuntary at the time, are a mark that we are not yet schooled in patience. How do I behave myself when these occasions arise?

The Divine Patience

When we speak of the patience of God we use the word in rather a different meaning to that in which it is applied to men. It means that God abstains from inflicting on the sinner the punishment that he deserves, that He is long-suffering, that He waits to see if he will perchance repent and turn to Him, that he is slow to anger and of great mercy. O my God, how patient You have been with me when I rebelled against You! How You have borne with all my ingratitude and sinfulness and stubbornness and disobedience!

Holy Scripture contains many examples of the patience of God. When the human family had become so wicked that God determined to destroy them by the Flood, He waited a hundred years before carrying out the sentence. When the cry of the Cities of the Plain rose up before Him He waited before He determined to destroy them. When Saul forfeited his kingdom by his disobedience, God waited for ten years before He carried out the sentence. Learn from God's example to be patient with evil-doers and to love mercy rather than vengeance.

God never acts in a hurry, and He thereby desires to teach us deliberation in all that we do. We do not leave an interval of time as He does between the wrong and the infliction of the punishment. We are so impulsive that we commit many faults that we might easily have avoided if we had learned to wait. What need was there for the delay that we find attributed to God? He, as perfect wisdom, needs no time for deliberation. But it is that we may recognise the necessity of being slow to act, and especially of being slow to act in anger, that God represents Himself as always waiting.

On Various Trials of Our Patience

Patience is tried by everything that puts an obstacle in the way of our action; by being kept waiting long; by having to repeat, over and over again, some lesson to a dull learner; by the perverse and wayward conduct of the young; by being interrupted while speaking when we have something we want to say; by a hundred similar incidents which continually occur. All these are a good test of our possession of this virtue. How do I stand the test in each case?

Our patience is also tried by those who misunderstand and misrepresent us. It is not easy to speak and think kindly of them. We are inclined either to avoid them or to show our dislike to them. We want to let them know what we think of them, and to give them a return blow for the blows we believe them to have given us. But patience bids us take the offence, real or supposed, quietly and without complaining; it checks the angry word and quenches the fire of resentment. Here, too, I have an excellent means of gauging my possession of this virtue.

Patience is also tried by poverty, sickness, desolation, loneliness, by uncongenial surroundings and employments which are not to our taste. We all have to suffer one or other of these painful circumstances of human existence. He who has the virtue of patience will bow his head and accept with ready acquiescence the trials that come to him. He will find plenty of good reasons why they have happened to him, and so far from regretting them or repining under them, he will say with the Psalmist: "For the Lord does not reject mankind for ever and ever. If He has punished, He has compassion so great is His kindness"; (*Lament* 3:31, 32).

The Mystery of Suffering

Those who look upon the world without taking into account the nature of sin, the meaning of a state of probation, and the rewards and punishments of the life to come, are puzzled by the sufferings that seem everywhere to abound. Why has a merciful God created us to suffer? Why is it that the innocent have to suffer while the guilty seem to prosper? Why is it that the most virtuous often have the hardest lot and the bitterest trials? Suffering is indeed a mystery.

Friendship with God generally entails suffering. How many a man hitherto prosperous falls into every kind of misfortune when he turns to God! It seems as if a high degree of virtue brought misery, not happiness. Dives surrounded with every luxury and Lazarus covered with ulcers lying half-starved at his gate; Annas triumphant and Jesus crucified; Herod feasting and John butchered in his prison cell; the Roman Emperor in all the pride of empire and the friends of God torn by wild beasts, what an apparent anomaly! On a small scale there is the same anomaly in my life and in the little world in which I live. I am inclined to find fault with God's arrangements. Oh how foolishly!

Does God repay good with evil by sending suffering to those he loves? They themselves do not think so, and they are the best judges. They rather like sufferings. How can this Be? Suffering in itself is the reverse of pleasant.

But in its effects how wonderful! In its power to counteract evil how effectual! As a mark of God's favour how valuable! In its promise for the future how replete with blessings! It may be said to contain within itself all sweetness, not in the present but in the future. This is the view I must take of suffering.

The Solution of the Mystery of Suffering

At the beginning there was no suffering. It was not until the angels rebelled that pain and suffering made their appearance in God's universe. Suffering is the necessary expiation of the outrage offered to the majesty of God by his creatures. It is a fulfilment of the eternal law that he who sins must suffer. It is the complement and effect of sin. It is the carrying out of the law of retribution. What else are my sufferings but the just punishment for my sins?

But suffering is a great deal more than this. It is the remedy for the disease of sin, the kindly knife that hurts but cures. What a change suffering makes in men. See Nebuchadnezzar before he suffered, proud and lifted up, and afterwards humble and submissive. (*Daniel* 4:27.) See the prodigal son led by suffering to return to his father's house. See even the wicked Achab humbled by suffering. (3 *Kings* 21:27.) "It is good, O Lord," says David, "that You have afflicted me. Before I was troubled I went wrong, but now I have kept Your word."

Chastisement yields to those who are exercised by it the peaceable fruit of justice. (*Hebrews* 12:11.) It purifies the soul, and almost forces men to humility and submission. Has it had this effect with me? If it has, I will thank God.

Suffering is the payment for joy to come. The willing acceptance of it is the surest road to a high place in Heaven. We can earn more grace for ourselves and for others by the patient endurance of suffering than by the most active zeal; it is a safer as well as a surer means of glorifying God, for we cannot well be proud of our sufferings as we may be of our actions. Thus it is one of the best gifts that God can give us. I therefore must be willing to pay the price if I desire to win the reward.

PATIENCE AND IMPATIENCE

The Praises of Patience

Patience is a virtue which receives in Holy Scripture, and especially in the writings of St Paul, praise almost without end. "He that is patient," says the Wise Man, "is governed with much wisdom." (*Prov* 14:29.) "Patience has a perfect work," says St James (ch. 1:4). "Patience is necessary to you," says St Paul, "that doing the will of God you may receive the promise." (*Hebrews* 10:36.) Think over these passages one by one, and question yourself whether you fulfil this necessary condition of eternal salvation.

Our Blessed Lord has Himself a special benediction for patience. "In your patience," He says, "you shall possess your souls." (*Luke* 2:19.) That is, by patience we shall save our souls. What higher praise could our Lord bestow upon patience than this? If it is to be the instrument of salvation, it is an inestimable treasure. Instead of dreading it, we ought to court it and welcome every occasion for its exercise. Every act of patience brings us nearer to Heaven, and the test of our fitness for the Kingdom of God is, have we learned to suffer with perfect patience?

St John does but echo the words of his Divine Master when he says (*Apoc* 7:14) of the redeemed around the throne, "These are they who came out of great tribulation." Not that the mere passing through suffering is sufficient, for he adds: "And have washed their robes and made them white in the Blood of the Lamb," that is, have obtained forgiveness by uniting their sufferings with the sufferings of the Son of God. Do I find in myself this description realised? Have I suffered and suffered willingly for Christ's sake? Or do I seek to avoid all suffering and fight against it, bear it impatiently when it comes?

The First Degree of Patience

When we are studying to acquire a virtue, it is generally the better plan to begin with external actions, and thence to proceed to the interior dispositions whence those actions proceed. In accordance with this rule, we must begin by repressing all signs of resentment and anger when we are offended, or when someone crosses our path, or hinders some work in which we are engaged. If under all this we can keep an unmoved and tranquil countenance, and avoid all expression of personal feeling and annoyance, this is a great point gained. Am I able to do this?

Why is it important to begin with exterior patience? First, because this helps enormously to calm the feelings within us just as we can work ourselves up into a fury by raging externally. Peace will soon return if we keep a serene face and quiet demeanour. Secondly, because exterior calmness under ill-usage edifies others and honours Christ our Lord, just as impatience and irritability disedify and dishonour the name of Christian. I must remember this when I am tempted to yield to my injured pride, and to retaliate on those who have offended me.

Our Lord Himself points out exterior patience as the first thing in which we should imitate Him, for He says: "Learn of Me, for I am meek and humble of heart." Meekness is but patience in its exterior manifestation. If I am sincere in my wish to follow in the footsteps of Christ my Lord, here is the best point with which to begin. I must for His sake and for love of Him be more gentle to those who give me pain, more tranquil under words and actions that wound or hurt me.

The Second Degree of Patience

The repression of external signs of impatience has no value in God's sight except in so far as it is a step to the interior virtue. The soldier, the courtier, the servant, suppresses the exterior marks of impatience for fear of punishment and hope of reward. The Christian must do more than this; he must have within him the motive of imitating the patience of Jesus Christ. Smoke is the sign of fire within, but the smoke will not warm the house unless there is the fire on the hearth; so external patience will not please God unless there is also the motive of patience within the soul. Am I striving after the interior virtue? Have I even succeeded in repressing the exterior impatience for Christ's sake?

When some unkindness or injury is done us, there arises in us a double feeling. We feel pained and hurt; in this there is no sort of sin. But we are also conscious of another feeling; a desire to retaliate, a wish to see some retribution befall the offender. We are bitter towards them, we are tempted to indulge ourselves in an animosity that approaches sometimes even to hatred. This is what has to be expelled from our souls if we are to resemble Him who was meek and humble of heart.

What must we do to rid ourselves of this bitterness? Dislike may remain in spite of all our efforts; this we cannot help. But we must resolve that no unkind wish towards the offender shall be indulged. Then we must set to work to pray for calmness and a spirit of forgiveness, then we must think of all we deserve for our offences against God, and must say from our heart: "Forgive us our trespasses as we forgive those who trespass against us." Last of all, we must pray for the offender.

The Third Degree of Patience

When we have succeeded in suppressing all outward impatience and inward resentment as far as it is voluntary and deliberate, we shall begin to reap the reward of our efforts. We shall find that the treatment which we once regarded as intolerable has certain advantages resulting from it. We may hope at last to find a positive pleasure in being overlooked or unfairly treated, in being humbled in the eyes of men, or blamed for what we did with all good intention. I must try to aim at this. It is not out of my reach.

How am I to gain this willingness to be misunderstood and harshly judged, this desire for rebuffs and disappointments? I must bring my common sense to bear on them. I must keep before myself how useful, how necessary for the beating down of pride. They are a most effectual means of making satisfaction for sin, if I offer them up to God in the name of Jesus Christ. When I remember all this, I ought to be quite anxious for what is a bitter but most salutary medicine.

When I read the lives of saints and holy men, I find there the true estimate of all things. Now, what was their attitude towards those who despised, persecuted, ill-treated them? They looked upon them as their greatest benefactors. How did they regard the reproaches, the neglect, the unkindness they had to undergo? They thanked God for them, rejoiced in them, considered it a misfortune if they were absent. If we want to resemble the saints, we must take their view of obloquy and misunderstanding. We must strive not only to put up with them but actually to welcome them, rejoice in them, consider them as our greatest privilege.

On Impatience

Impatience is one of the most foolish of all faults. It gains nothing for us; it does not relieve our sufferings, but aggravates them. No one enjoys any peace as long as he is yielding to feelings of impatience; he is discontented, miserable, uneasy. He finds intolerable what he could bear well enough if only he would make the necessary effort, and gulp down the rising irritation or suppress the angry words. He is always in a fever, and is a nuisance to himself and to all around him. Do not I know this by experience? If not, I must thank God for giving me so happy a disposition.

Impatience is also one of the most ridiculous of all faults. There is something laughable and contemptible in the fuming of the impatient man over some trifle, in his rage because he cannot overcome some difficulty or have his own way as he desires. An impatient man always makes a bad impression. If I could see myself as others see me when I give way to impatience, I should be thoroughly ashamed and very careful not to make myself so foolish again.

Impatience, when voluntarily indulged, is a sort of indirect rebellion against God. It is a practical refusal to bear willingly the trials that He has laid upon us; it is kicking against the goad. No wonder that we hurt ourselves in so doing; it is only what we deserve. We all of us need trials, but if instead of profiting by them and learning patience from them, they are to us only an occasion of impatience, they simply increase our condemnation. If I give way to impatience, it shows that I am not subject as I ought to be to the law of God, and still less to the sweet yoke of Christ.

On Physical Impatience

Physical impatience is that involuntary feeling of irritation which is aroused in us by some external and physical cause. We are looking for something and cannot find it. We are trying to fix our thoughts, and some distracting noise renders it impossible. We are trying to compose ourselves to sleep, and some troublesome neighbour wakes us up just as slumber was creeping over us. On account of all such impatience we should humble ourselves, as being a sign of faults indulged in the past, not of present sin.

This sort of physical impatience anticipating our reason is very often the result of impatience, pride, self-will long indulged. The ghost of past sins reappearing to remind us of what we have forgotten and to keep us humble. Not always, for St Teresa tells us that owing to ill-health and desolation, she had the greatest difficulty in remaining calm and gentle and in resisting the impulse to speak sharply and disagreeably. But as a general rule, such physical impatience may be taken, at all events while we are in good health, as a mark of pride not completely subdued, and of self-will that has not fully learned to submit.

How are we to be rid of physical impatience? Chiefly by schooling ourselves to endure by bearing willingly even what we could avoid, by waiting long before we knock again, if our first signal produces no effect, by checking the word of complaint or gesture indicative of our suffering. Such little efforts at self-mastery are very pleasing to God; they often cost us a good deal. They may be concerned with trifles, but the victory over ourselves is no trifle. Learn then to seek to overcome the first movements of physical impatience.

On Complaining

When anything pains or annoys us, it is a natural impulse to relieve our feelings by telling our griefs to others, partly from a hope of sympathy, partly because it is a great relief to express our vexation or our sorrow. Such complaints are rarely made without sin. It is scarcely possible to speak of what we have suffered without some breach of the law of charity. We must strive to exercise the virtue of patience, and check the rising words in which we are about to pour forth the story of our wrongs.

The effort of keeping silent in such a case soon brings its reward. The pain after a time diminishes, whereas to have dilated on it would have made us feel more bitterly than before. Those who know that we have suffered are edified by our silence. Our wrong-doer is often won over by our meekness. Peace comes into our heart. Do I suppress for Christ's sake and to imitate His patience, unkind words rising to my lips? When I have done so, do I not find that patience brings its own reward?

Yet this does not mean that I am always to bury my griefs in my own heart. Sometimes I cannot do so; out they will come in spite of my efforts. Sometimes it is almost a duty to tell our story to some kind and sympathising friend; half of our troubles disappear or are sensibly diminished in the mere act of telling. But we must choose one whom we can trust and respect. We must be careful not to speak bitterly or to abuse others by way of venting our feelings. We must try to excuse others, and must tell our story simply and with all charity. Do I observe this rule when I am pouring my troubles into the ear of some friend or adviser?

TEMPTATION

The Endurance of Temptation

Temptations are a necessary element in the career of all the servants of God. "Because you were acceptable to God," says the Angel to Tobias, "it was necessary that temptation should try you." (*Tobias* 12:13.) Temptations, therefore, far from being any mark of God's anger or displeasure, are a sign of His love and favour. This ought to be our consolation when we are harassed by temptations. St James tells us: "My brothers, you will always have your trials but, when they come, try to treat them as a happy privilege" (*James* 1:2.) I must take a more cheerful view of temptation than I have hitherto done. I must take it as a mark of God's favour, and then I shall meet it more bravely.

How is temptation a sign of God's love? It is an excellent instrument for engendering humility. If we are inclined to think too much of ourselves, nothing brings us to our senses like some humiliating temptation. It shows us our own weakness and the necessity of continual reliance on God. It produces in us a spirit of dependence upon God. This is the only way to pass through temptation safely. God has promised that He will always make a way to escape from every temptation.

Temptation is also necessary to enable us to feel for others under their temptations. Even our Lord, the Apostle tells us, suffered being tempted, that He may be able to succour those that are tempted. (*Hebrews* 2:18.) He knew indeed from the beginning all that His servants suffer, but by enduring temptation He learned it by His own experience so as to feel their sufferings. We do not even know the sufferings of others, much less can we sympathise with them thoroughly. Am I gentle towards those who are tempted, or am I hard and unsympathetic?

Patience under Temptations

If we all have to endure temptations, we must try to endure them well. Temptations are not sins. We may be surrounded with temptations. They may be present to us for hours. We may have a sort of guilty feeling as if we had offended God. Yet if we are not conscious of having in any way consented to them, if throughout we have wished them away, then our conscience is free from any stain of sin, even though they may have caused satisfaction to our lower nature and to our baser inclinations. To remember this will help us not a little in bearing them patiently.

But there is another consoling consideration with respect to temptation. We may do much for the honour of

God and for our own progress in virtue by our resistance to the tempter. We lay up a store of merit in Heaven. We are purified as in the fire, and the dross of venial sins and imperfections is taken away. We must therefore be not only patient, but cheerful under temptations, and thank God for them.

Some of the greatest saints were subject to terrible temptations. St Paul, who had been rapt to the third Heaven, was tempted by the sting of the flesh; St Alphonsus, by doubts against every article of the Faith, by vanity, presumption, and concupiscence; St Rose, by darkness, and a seeming hopelessness of being saved; she felt no love of God and feared that she was already among the lost. Yet these were great saints, and they proved their sanctity by their faithfulness under temptation, by crying out, "Jesus, forsake me not! In You, O Lord, I have trusted, let me not be confounded for ever." I will do the same: I will never lose hope, I will never lose my confidence in God.

On Patience in Sickness

It is not easy for those who have always enjoyed robust health to understand how heavy a cross is a long-continued sickness. It is not merely the physical pain, though this is often very hard to bear. It is the discomfort, the weariness. the languor, the depression, that accompany sickness; it is the restlessness, the inability to find repose, the loneliness of the long hours. What need the sick have of patience! Patience should be the watchword of their life. Grant me patience, O Lord, patience to suffer for You and with You, and never to murmur even when the pain and suffering is greatest.

There is a form of ill-health which is the hardest of all to bear with patience; when we go about our usual occupations in a state of suffering that makes everything a burden. We get little sympathy because we are still able to do our work, or perhaps we are blamed because we are not able to do it well. Oh, what compassion we should have for those who suffer thus, and if it is our own lot, we should do our best to unite our sufferings with the sufferings of Jesus and ask Him to grant us patience to carry our heavy cross.

We sometimes fancy that when we are ill and unable to do active work for God, we are useless and cannot gain graces for ourselves or for others. This is a great mistake; we can gain more graces in sickness than in health. Suffering is more pleasing to God than doing; it earns greater merit, it prepares us more speedily for heaven, it blots out sin more rapidly. Many of the saints were sanctified by sickness. Hence bear it willingly, try and rejoice in it.

Patience under Bereavement

Pure human love, especially the love of father and mother for their children, is one of the most beautiful things in the natural order. It interweaves itself with our very nature. Husband and wife, brother and sister, and above all the children who are in a special sense our own, are a part of ourselves; they are our own by birth, our own by constant association, our own by a thousand ties of love. Oh, how hard it is to lose one of our little circle, to see the empty place, to miss their looks of love, the sweet sound of their voice. Then indeed we have need of patience, and must beg that we may not grieve like those who have no hope, but may humbly bow our necks under God's chastising hand.

Patience! how are we to obtain it under the crushing blow? How are we to recognise the love of God in thus taking away the light of our eyes from us? It is indeed hard, and for a time the absorbing grief may overpower us. But we can always pray, we can always make an act of resignation, we can always say: "Not as I will, but as You will." "It is the Lord, let Him do what is good in His sight." Has this been my conduct when one whom I dearly loved was taken from me?

There are many motives of consolation when friends and dear ones fade away or die. If they died in their innocence, how we ought to rejoice when we think of them with Christ in Heaven! If they had sinned and done penance we ought to rejoice that God gave them the grace of dying a good death. We can always console ourselves by praying for them. We can make their departure a reason for living a better and a holier life, that we may not fail of meeting them again before the throne of God. All this I will do more from now on.

On Patience under Contempt

There are few things so hard for human nature to bear as contempt. To be regarded as not worthy of notice, to be spoken of in terms implying that we are looked down upon, to be passed over as if of no importance in the eyes of others, all this is indeed painful to us and sorely tries our patience. When I am thus treated, how do I take it? Am I desirous to prove my importance and the necessity of considering me? If so, I shall not have the patience that I ought to have. I still have much of the spirit of pride left in me. I must pray God to make me more humble.

Why is it that contempt is so painful to us? It is because our natural craving is after power and influence. We do not realise our own insignificance. If we did we should be quite willing to be overlooked. We should dislike the high esteem of men. This was the case with the saints. They shunned honour and courted contempt. St Philip used to go into the Cardinals' places in St Peter's on a *festa* that he might have the humiliation of being thrust out. St Francis used to kneel down in the refectory and openly accuse himself of gluttony. Oh my God! shall I ever obtain this grace of being satisfied to be despised, and of disliking to be honoured?

What would be the treatment bestowed upon us if those around us saw us as we are in God's sight, if they knew all the wicked thoughts and sinful actions of our past life? What would be their estimate of us if they saw us with all the abominations of our soul unveiled; if they beheld our pride, and selfishness, and sloth, and impurity, and self-indulgence, our high esteem of ourselves and our indifference to God? Oh how they would despise us then! How we ought to despise ourselves!

Some Motives for Patience under Contempt

It is always foolish to complain or to be dissatisfied with that which of its own nature is calculated to advance our happiness and our highest interests. Contempt is better suited than almost anything else to humble us, if we take it as we ought. It cannot fail to tear up the pride that is so deeply rooted in our hearts and which is the great obstacle between us and God. Ought we not then to be grateful to those who do us this service? Instead of resenting this treatment of us, we ought to thank God and pray for them as our benefactors.

When we look into ourselves, must we not acknowledge that contempt is what ought to be felt towards us? It is the fitting disposition, the proper attitude towards one so contemptible as I am. My love of what is fitting ought to make me welcome it as the right and proper thing. I ought not only to acquiesce in it, but to be pleased at justice being done to me. I ought to say to myself when treated with contempt, That is just and right! It is exactly the true view to take of me!

Above all, I ought to value contempt because it gives me a share in the humiliation of my dear Lord and Saviour Jesus Christ. He humbled Himself even to death. He was treated with the utmost contempt and ignominy by the very creatures He had made, who owed all to Him, and on whom He had bestowed countless benefits and lavished unmeasured love. What can be better or happier or a greater privilege than thus to be clad in the livery of my Lord, and to be treading, all unworthy as I am, in His footsteps? Welcome then contempt and ignominy for Jesus' sake and as giving me a share in His Divine life.

EXAMPLES OF PATIENCE

The Patience of Job

The patience of Job is proverbial. It is held up in Holy Scripture for our imitation. (*James* 5:11.) It was commended by God Himself and received a rich reward even in this world. It is therefore worthy of our study and imitation.

The patience of Job supported him not against one kind of misfortune only, but against a series of all kinds of calamities coming upon him one after another in rapid succession. All his goods were taken from him, and his children were one and all killed by the fall of a house where they were. Job, so far from murmuring, simply worshiped God, saying: "The Lord gave and the Lord has taken away: Blessed be the name of the Lord!" Is this my language when I suffer?

Job's next misfortune befell his own body. He was smitten with grievous ulcers from head to foot. His wife, seeing his condition, cried out to him that it was better to put an end to his life than to live on in such a state. But Job gently reproved her: "If we have received good things at the hand of the Lord, why should we not receive evil?"

I too have received good things without number from God's hand. Shall I then murmur if I receive a little of the evil of which I have deserved so much?

But this was not the end of Job's troubles. His three friends came to comfort him, and began to taunt him as a vain man lifted up by pride, who had hardened his heart and thus brought all this misery upon himself. Poor Job could not retrain the expression of his misery; he poured forth words of sorrow, yet he never lost his patience or his confidence in God. Do I thus keep up my trust in God when all around fail or reproach me undeservedly? Am I gentle and patient with them as was Job?

The Source of Job's Patience

How was it that Job was able to bear with patience his manifold calamities? It was not that he did not feel them acutely, or that he wrapped himself in a mantle of self-reliant pride. It was simply due to his great subservience to the will of God. His motto was: "As it has pleased the Lord, so let it be done." He was quite satisfied with whatever was the Divine good pleasure, and so whatever happened he could say from his heart, Blessed be the name of the Lord; he could thank God for it, however great the pain and misery resulting to himself.

There was a further secret of Job's patience. He placed his hopes of happiness in the future, not in the present: "I know that my Redeemer lives, I know that in my flesh I shall see God." When a man thus realises the love of Jesus, and is able to say my Redeemer (as St Paul said, He loved me and gave Himself for me), he has amid all his troubles a source of consolation that never can dry up. He is able to look to the joyful day of the resurrection. In my trials I must thus look to Jesus, and think of the reward to come which shall richly compensate for all present pain.

Job was not only perfectly resigned but ready for fresh sufferings if it were God's will and if no rebellion in his heart should follow from the additional calamities. "Let this be my comfort that afflicting me He spare not, and that I may not contradict the words of the Holy One." Is this my spirit? Have I the generosity to pray for more sufferings and more humiliations? At least I will pray that God may send me whatever He sees will cleanse me from sin, and help me to love Him more.

The Reward of Job's Patience

"You have heard of the patience of Job, and understood the Lord's purpose, realising that the Lord is kind and compassionate." (*James* 5:11.)

The patience of Job produced as its first-fruit humility. Though he had never lost his patience nor in any way rebelled against God, yet when he heard the voice of God declaring to him the Divine Majesty, he accuses himself of speaking unwisely of things that exceeded his knowledge. "I reprehend myself and do penance in dust and ashes." This is the effect of suffering on the friends of God; it does not embitter them, it humbles them.

Job earned the approval of God Himself as having spoken aright. Against his friends the wrath of God was kindled for their unkindness, their rash judgment, their censorious words. They were commanded to offer sacrifice for their sins and to ask Job to pray for them if they desired to escape God's anger. Thus God will always justify His faithful servants, if they leave their cause in His hands. "Blessed are those who wait for Him, they will not be disappointed." Is this my policy, or am I keen to fight my own battles?

God rewarded Job even in this life for his patience. One by one his relations came to comfort him and bring him presents. God blessed His flocks, his herds, his family, and be became doubly as rich as ever. Sons and daughters grew up around him, and Job was happy and prosperous. He died at last, full of days, leaving behind him a name to be honoured as an example of patience as long as the world lasts, and receiving in Heaven a rich reward. Am I earning by my patience in this life God's blessing and an eternal reward in Heaven?

The Patience of Mary

As Jesus came to suffer, it was necessary that Mary should suffer with Him. This was her greatest privilege, and she knew it to be such. She knew it even when her human love broke forth in the words of expostulation: "Son, why have You so dealt with us?" She knew it when she stood broken-hearted beneath the Cross. She knew it when she received in her arms the Body of her Son after He had been taken down from the Cross. She knew from first to last that the best proof of our Lord's love is to give us a share in His sufferings. This was Mary's consolation; is it mine when I have to suffer?

We do not read much in Holy Scripture respecting the patience of Mary, but enough to know that Jesus purposely tried her patience. Why did He prompt holy Simeon to pierce her heart with the prediction of her coming sufferings? Why did He compel her to start in the dark night on the journey to Egypt, when He could so easily have defeated Herod's projects? Why did He not let her know where He was when he remained behind in Jerusalem? Why did He apparently rebuke her at the marriage of Cana? Why did He allow her heart to be torn by the sight of His Crucifixion? It was all that she might have a more glorious reward and share His triumph in a greater degree.

If we could have seen Mary upon earth, we should have been especially struck by her undisturbed peace. This was owing to her perfect patience and readiness to accept everything at God's hand. "Behold the handmaid of the Lord; let it be done to me according to your word." If I desire peace, this must be the motto of my life.

The Patience of Jesus Christ

As in all other virtues, so in patience Jesus Christ is our Teacher and Example. None ever suffered as He did, and therefore none had to exercise such patience as He exercised.

How patient He was with those who reviled and abused Him! Never one indignant word, never one angry look, nothing but sweetness and kindness. "Father, forgive them, for they know not what they do." Oh, when shall I be able to imitate the patience of Jesus! when shall I approach even at a distance the Divine Model I profess to imitate!

How patient He was with His Apostles! How their roughness, selfishness, stupidity, must have jarred upon Him! They misunderstood His words, they quarrelled among themselves, His predictions respecting the Passion fell upon deaf ears, they all forsook Him in time of danger yet He never was ruffled by the faintest breath of anger or impatience. He who was the Infinite God put up with their inconstancy, selfishness, ambition. Once more, how far am I from the gentleness and patience of the Son of God!

In the midst of physical agony such as none other ever tasted, how patient He was! Nothing save a gentle moaning expressive of the agony He was enduring escaped His lips when the scourges lacerated His Sacred

Body, and when the nails were driven through His hands and feet. He endured what even He could not have borne had He not been God, and used His Divinity to enable Him to suffer more. Yet He was always submissive to the will of God, always taking a sort of strange joy in His acutest agony, because He knew the rich reward at hand, the long-lived seed who through Him would be redeemed from the wrath of God and endless misery.

The Patience of the Saints

To the grace of patience all the saints in great measure owe their eternal reward. Their crown in Heaven will not be due so much to what they have done for God as to what they have suffered for Him. In them "patience has its perfect work" (*James* 1:4), and that work has been to prepare them for the eternal joys of Heaven. Oh, how grateful they will be to God for the patience that He has given them to suffer willingly for Him! How grateful they will be for the sufferings that have procured for them such happiness inexpressible and peace that knows no end.

The saints while still on earth have a truer view of all the events of life than we have. They value above all things, even while they are still suffering them, the crosses and afflictions that God sends them. The Apostles counted it joy to suffer shame for Christ's sake. "We glory in tribulation," says St Paul. St Francis Xavier prayed for more suffering; St Teresa that she might go on suffering until her death. This was no mere sentiment, it was common sense and ordinary prudence. They found a real joy even here in suffering. Have I any such joy? Or do I dislike and try to avoid suffering? Here is a test of whether I am like the saints.

The patience of the saints was more severely tried than is ours. Not only were they stoned, racked, torn asunder, not only did they suffer want, distress, afflictions (*Hebrews* 11:37), but they had to endure what was still harder, ingratitude, failure, unkindness, false accusations, desolation, darkness. Yet they willingly endured all for Jesus' sake - never ceasing to love Him through it all. I have my trials, yet none so dreadful as those, yet I complain even under my lighter cross.

The Patience of the Martyrs

To lay down one's life for Christ is one of the greatest honours that can be bestowed upon us. It ensures an immediate entrance into Heaven. It gives us a part, such as nothing else can give, in the sufferings of Him who laid down His life for us. It is a crowning mark of God's mercy to those who are His special friends. It is not in the power of all who desire it; it is given to those for whom God has destined it and to none else. It has to be purchased by a long course of faithful service of God. If only God would give me such a privilege how happy I should be. If only I could live so as to deserve it!

Even the weak, the timid, the sensitive, can, if God gives them the special grace of martyrdom, face undismayed the most cruel tortures. Sometimes they did not feel the pain even when it was most agonising. The secret joy of their hearts at the thought that they were suffering for Christ made it seem light to them, and gave them fortitude to endure it to the end. If God should at any time give me the happiness of dying for Him, He will take away all the fear and will give me a light and joyous heart even in the midst of the greatest physical sufferings.

If there is little or no prospect of my laying down my life for Christ, yet I can at least make the offering to Him; I can present myself to suffer anything that He has in store for me. It may be that I am destined for suffering worse than death in the prolonged martyrdom of physical or mental anguish. But one thing I know, that He will never lay upon me suffering beyond what I am able to bear, and will with the suffering give the grace necessary to endure it with resignation and perhaps even with joy.

The Patience of the Angels

Patience is an angelical virtue as well as purity. The patience of our Guardian Angels must sometimes be sorely tried. Oh, how often they give advice which is not listened to, and whisper into the ear of their clients messages from God, but speak to ears that are wilfully deaf! How often they warn us, but we neglect their warnings! How little notice we take of them and how ungrateful we are to them for all their care! Even when we pray, and in answer to our prayer our Guardian Angel signifies to us what God desires us to do, we often turn away and follow our own perverse inclinations instead. Have I not too often done so?

There is nothing more trying to the patience of those who have active energetic natures than to be continually thwarted, to fail through the obstinacy and stupidity and willfulness of others, to see their plans fail without any fault of their own. What can be the effect upon the Guardian Angels when one plan after another that they devise for our good fails, and when we thwart their endeavours and render all their efforts fruitless when we throw away grace after grace and they know that these graces never will return. Is it not enough to cause them to relinquish such clients in disgust?

Yet their charity and patience never fail. When we neglect one grace they obtain another for us. When we do that which offends God they pray for us all the more. Untiringly they devise means for bringing us to our senses and never give over their efforts as long as life endures. They are thus our model in dealing with perverse sinners; never to lose heart or be cast down by failure, but to go on to the end patiently working and praying.

The Patience of the Holy Souls

In Purgatory the suffering is more intense than any suffering of this present life and therefore there is greater need of patience to endure it. But the Holy Souls have their wills in perfect conformity to the will of God, and they cannot be anything but patient amid their torments. They do not and they cannot rebel, but their submission does not remove the bitterness of their unceasing sorrow, as they think how comparatively easy it would have been for them to avoid while still on earth their present anguish by greater faithfulness to grace and by uniting their actions and sufferings to the actions and sufferings of the Divine Son of God.

If we could look forward to those sufferings with an appreciation of what they are, how patient we should be now! We should consider it a privilege to suffer now as the very best way of avoiding the agony of that fire which will be kindled by the wrath of God, and will in some way correspond to our ingratitude and unfaithfulness to our King and Benefactor. If no other motive makes me patient under my earthly sufferings, yet at least the prospect of long years of far worse sufferings ought to make me choose the lighter suffering now. What am I doing to shorten my Purgatory?

The Holy Souls must sometimes think reproachfully how little their friends on earth do to help them. Among many other methods of aiding them, I can offer up for them all the pains of mind and body that God sends me, asking God to accept it in alleviation of their sufferings. This will help me to be patient and to suffer willingly, and when my time comes I shall find that patient suffering for others will shorten my time of banishment from God in the fires of Purgatory.

Fruits of Patience

The First Fruit of Patience: Peace

We all long after peace; we are anxious not for inactivity,
nor indeed that we should have nothing against which to
fight, but for the absence of that conflict within us which
is the source of all our misery. It is the struggle in our
own hearts between two opposing forces of duty and
inclination that troubles and disturbs us. If this struggle is
to cease, one of these two forces must be crushed. It is the
process of crushing our corrupt inclinations that we
dread. We have not the necessary courage, though we
know that the only way to peace is to mortify our
members which are upon the earth. This is the story of
my troubles, I have not conquered my lower nature and
my self-will.

How is the victory to be gained and peace restored to
our hearts? It is impossible without suffering. Nothing
else has the power to break our proud wills and make us
put our stubborn necks beneath the yoke. We speak of
those who have suffered having a chastened look, and it
always attracts us. There is in suffering a sort of magic
which ought to commend it to us, or at least to reconcile

us to it. If I have to suffer, I will think of this, and console myself with knowing that God will bring peace and happiness out of it.

But it is not all suffering that has this wholesome effect, but only suffering borne with patience. If we are impatient, rebellious, unresigned, our suffering may be an occasion of fresh trouble rather than of peace. I must accept it from the hand of God, if it is to bring with it that quiet tranquillity which I have never yet attained as I ought. I must bow my head and place myself in God's hands to suffer as He pleases, whatever He pleases, as long as he pleases. This is the only road to solid peace.

The Second Fruit of Patience: Hope

"Sufferings," says St Paul, " bring patience, as we know, and patience brings perseverance, and perseverance brings hope." (*Romans* 5:4.) If we humbly accept the sufferings God sends us without rebellion or complaint, then we reap the reward in a rapid growth of hope within our heart. Through the darkness we descry a bright light in the distance, and though our path be a dreary and a painful one, this prospect cheers us up and makes us go on our way rejoicing. In the earlier part of the time of trial, hope was dim and faint, but when we have been proved faithful servants, hope begins to anticipate the future and to fill us with a happiness which makes the present sufferings comparatively light. Have I attained that happy state?

Joined to this prospect of the future is a great confidence in God in the present. Confidence is a part of hope. When we have learned by patience to trust Him amid sorrow, tribulation, disappointment, then we have a solid foundation for trusting Him all the rest of our lives, not only with a sort of blind assurance that all he does is best, but with a consciousness of the happy results to come from all that patience bids us bear, results, too, which we begin to experience even here. I must then aim at this confidence and pray that I may gain it by patience.

St Paul tells us that if we hope for that which we see not, we have to wait for it, for the perfect work of patience is to wait contentedly for the time when God will give us the good things He has promised us. This was the Apostle's frame of mind when he said: "I have fought a good fight, I have kept the faith, at the last there is laid up for me a crown of justice." (*2 Timothy* 4:7.) So, too, for me, if I persevere to the end, there is laid up a like crown. The thought of it shall animate me to fresh patience.

The Third Fruit of Patience: Joy

"As it were sorrowing yet always rejoicing." (*2 Cor* 6:10.) This is St Paul's description of the ministers of Christ, labouring for the salvation of souls. What is true of them is true of all faithful servants of God. On the surface apparent misery, but down in the depths of the soul intense joy. Of this joy St Paul says: "In all our trouble I am filled with consolation and my joy is overflowing". (*2 Cor* 7:4.) What is it that works this charm? Patience. Patient endurance, humble submission to the will of God, resignation to His providence.

How is it that out of sorrow joy can come? The reason is that if we are living for God and in dependence on Him, and seeking to promote His glory, then, although in the natural order we may be crushed down with pain and suffering, we shall be full of joy by reason of the supernatural gladness that God bestows on us. "Your joy," says our Lord to His Apostles, "no man shall take from you." (*John* 16:22.) Have I any experience of this joy? If so, I will thank God for it; if not, I must wait patiently, and see whether there may not be some hindrance to it on my part.

Whence comes this joy? From Heaven. This is why it surpasses all earthly joy and makes earthly sufferings sweet. It is the first faint reflection of the light of Heaven amid the clouds and darkness of earth; the first foretaste of the joy into which the just will be welcomed by their Lord at the gate of Heaven. If one drop of it on earth sweetens all bitterness, and makes all sufferings light, what must be the intensity of joy which will inebriate all those who have here endured tribulation and suffering for Christ's sake?

Hope in Adversity

This book gives guidance and encouragement to those going through a period of suffering. It offers the Word of God from Scripture as a divine source of inspiration, light and hope, together with writings from popular spiritual masters, and thoughtful reflections. It reflects on Faith, Patience, Prayer, Trust, Obedience and Hope in suffering. This little book of comfort counsels us not to fear, but to make a companion of wisdom, to pray confidently to the loving Father, to trust in God's will in the everyday things, and to live with courageous hope.

ISBN: 978 1 86082 148 6

CTS Code: D656